# LET'S MAKE AMERICA GREAT AGAIN—

## *LIKE NORWAY!*

Dr. Bob O'Connor

2019

Total Health Publications

TABLE OF CONTENTS

## PREFACE

Many Americans, following Donald Trump, think that America is not great. They seem to want more and better jobs, fewer immigrants, better and cheaper health care, lower taxes, and a return to "that old time religion." It doesn't seem to matter much about the leader's personal morality, as long as he says he is against abortions and Muslims.

Donald Trump said he would like to see more Norwegians immigrate to America. But his demeanor seems to be dissuading them from coming. U.S. universities were once the preferred destinations for college educations for "Nordmen." This is no longer true. Modern young Vikings are turning to other countries for their tertiary schooling.

"The Donald," as many other leaders, sees Norway as a rather special country. What is it that makes it special. Let's take a look! Let's also look at a few critical areas, like pensions and taxes, and see if we can make a few moves toward being better.

While Norway will be our key interest, some other countries have enacted some laudable programs. But ironically none of their national leaders are advocating building walls along their borders or blaming Barack Obama for their real or imagined past mistakes.

# **INTRODUCTION**

Everybody seems to love Norway. Bernie Sanders wants to develop America along the same lines as Scandinavia, and Trump wants more Norwegians to emigrate to the United States. Although I wonder if "The Donald" would be comfortable with the gender equality he would find here and if he would be ready to have Americans pay 60% more in taxes (from 26% to 42%) just to be in a happier country, and one that was low on corruption and rated as the best democracy in the world by the Economist Intelligence Unit.

The U.S. is rated the 21st best democracy. No wonder Trump keeps harping on the idea of making America great again. But first he has to pass Uruguay at number 18 and Canada at number 6 on his way to tying with Norway as the world's best democracy!

Transparency International ranked 180 countries on their scale of corruption. Norway was ranked as the third least corrupt and U.S. the 16th least corrupt.

On the other hand, the U.S. has been ranked sixth on the ease of doing business scale of the World Bank. Norway ranked eighth. New Zealand was first. (New Zealand is also the 6th happiest country and the fourth best democracy, but its total taxes are 37%!)

But there may be other factors than business and taxes. Did you know that Norway has some of the best chefs in the world? The Bocuse d'Or, called the Olympics of gastronomic cooking, was inaugurated in 1987 and is held biennially. Norway has won more medals than any other country—5 golds, 3 silvers, and 2 bronzes. The U.S. has one gold and one silver. By comparison, France has 7 golds and one each of silver and bronze. Belgium, another capitol of cuisine has no golds, but three each of silver and bronze. And who would have guessed that two years ago a cheese from Norway was ranked as the best in the world? What a wily lot these socialists!

But back to money. Are Americans ready to pay more taxes to be happier, to have a more effective democracy, to have less corruption, and no national debt? Every American now owes about $70,000 on the national debt. By contrast, Norwegians each have a share of the trillion dollar Norwegian Wealth Fund—they each are worth $190,000 because of it. How do they do it? In Norway the people own the oil under the ground and under their ocean. In the U.S. billionaires own the oil.

Americans are continually fooled when the government gives them tax breaks—then borrows money to fund them. Of course, we then pay interest annually on that national debt. Boy, are we smart!

After living in California, where I was a conservative Republican, then moving to Norway for 25 years, I became a liberal Democrat. Part of the metamorphosis was seeing how the two countries worked, and part was my disgust with the way that many Republicans often resorted to propaganda, lies during the election process, their unfair gerrymandering of voting districts, their barring many eligible voters from their polling places, and their reliance in their political messaging on unconscious motivations such as fear and anger rather than on a civilized discussion of the real issues and how that could be best realized.

George W. Bush and Donald Trump were examples of the first, while John McCain was an example of the intellectual type of appeal. But the intelligent arguments of McCain lost, while the appeals to anger and fear of Bush and Trump won for them. In Norway, these psychological appeals would have been losers. Norwegians vote on the real issues—not because they are scare-mongered into the voting booth.

Advertisers, successful politicians, and other practical psychologists know that we are primarily motivated through our unconscious minds. On the other hand, our Founding Fathers were outstanding examples of people being directed by their intellects. Many people will give considerable thought to whom they will elect and what propositions are good for the country. It is a sad commentary that so many Americans are practically illiterate and can think no farther ahead than their last auditory injection from the right or the left-wing politicians or pundits.

My experience in talking with American workers and middle-class managers is that they are far less aware of the issues in America than are the tradesman in Norway. The typical Norwegian reads at least one newspaper a day and listens to the televised news at 7 o'clock. They are also likely to listen to the debates on television that may clarify national issues. In short, they are more interested and informed citizens on issues and problems both in Norway and in America.

Since my first extended travel to Europe in 1962, I have seen a large number of changes. The idea of the equality of all people has erased the traditional ideas of a permanently stratified society as we have seen in monarchies and other authoritarian regimes that have enslaved Europeans at least since the age of Rome.

While the idea of pensions can be traced back to the German Chancellor Otto von Bismarck, in 1881, it took a few years for the idea to become law. Earlier, in some European countries, there had been laws that gave a pittance to the poor. But Bismarck made us think about the needs of productive citizens.

The U.S. finally caught up with Europe in pension rights in 1936 with its Social Security Act. (A worker could retire at 65, but our life expectancy then was 64!)

That was the same year that France mandated 12 paid vacation days. The U.S. still has no federal mandate for a vacation, or a paid vacation. While Norwegians enjoy four to six weeks of paid vacation and ten national holidays, they also get an additional month's pay in December and extra pay in June for their vacation.

There are so many areas that we can compare. We can look at the economic systems, political systems, how the two countries are concerned with developing strong families, their healthcare systems, what is it that makes people happy, and a number of other areas. After we do this we will take a step behind the obvious workings of the governments and look at the "whys" that have caused or resulted from the basic assumptions of the two countries.

# CHAPTER 1
# WHAT  SHOULD BE A GOVERNMENT'S MAJOR CONCERN

The welfare of the people from cradle to grave is one option. Another would be to aid the rich to make and keep more money. Another would be to consolidate power in the king or the ruling party. We see all of these in varying proportions today. Just look at Norway, the U.S., and Saudi Arabia as obvious examples.

The United States is a conservative country. It conserves the value of faith in the unknowable.   You can believe in just about anything and have your beliefs affirmed by the courts. In terms of business, making money is the major concern. It conserves the values of capitalism. The tax codes give thousands of possibilities for deducting expenses from one's income. As a result, some major companies pay very little income tax, and some pay none.

Some businesses are aided by sweet tax avoidance deals by state and local governments, at taxpayer expense. Businesses employ some local people so it helps the community, but they lose the business or property taxes. Walt Disney, Marriott, and Lockheed Martin are just a handful of companies that have done this.

We can assume that in primitive peoples, the family or the clan were primary and most people were seen as important. Infants were probably particularly important. When the men hunted a deer, the meat was shared.

As societies and civilizations developed, stratification became more evident. Some people were kings, some were slaves. Some people were gladiators whose death was a spectacle, a moment of grief. Rulers seem to have had little respect for the serfs and soldiers that sustained them.

It seems that around the 16th and 17th centuries, whether because of religion or empathy, the poor people were becoming recognized as "human" and laws developed that often paid a pittance to the poor and disabled. Bismarck expanded that concern for the elderly. The developing use of democracy as a preferred form of government seemed to expand the idea of some Enlightenment thinkers that people were somehow equal-- and even that their needs were equal.

In the 19th century, Karl Marx went much further in castigating laissez-faire capitalism and proposing the society that must eventually emerge-- communism. Communism held the ideal that "from each according to his ability, to each according to his needs."

As the earlier revolutions in France and America developed, the idea of equality of all people became a battle cry as kings were dispatched or their power diminished. But as the American Constitution and the French the Declaration of the Rights of Man evolved, liberty rather than equality became the dominant value for a society. While equal rights had been proclaimed during those revolutions, the United Nations and the European Union have expanded on those equal rights. But equal rights don't suggest that people are equal, only that they have equal access to some liberties.

Political philosophers are well aware that the concepts of "equality" and "liberty" are often antithetical. When one person has the freedom to make as much money as possible and another person wants to share that wealth because he has an equal right to income equality-- one or the other of these political ideals must be minimized.

In the US, liberty and individual responsibility hold a dominant place in politics. This makes the U.S. quite conservative when compared to most European countries. This conservative leaning is clearly shown: in the principles of the Republican Party, in the number of religious people in the country, and, in the concern for lower taxes. People, like the President, don't want climate change to be true-- so it isn't. They want to believe in the religions of their parents. New ideas are often accepted as true, if they can bolster older beliefs.

For example, the idea that the soul is put into the ovum at the instant of conception of a human being has only been true since 1869 when Pope Pius IX said it was true. (Before 1869 the religious beliefs held through high school that "personhood" occurred sometime between the 5th week of pregnancy and birth—depending on your sect.) Because of this relatively new pronouncement, people must have children that they don't want and society should be taxed $120,000 to pay for their education and whatever other expenses that might occur in their lifetimes. Strangely, the conservatives now want unwanted children to be born and taxes to be raised to pay for them—while also wanting lower taxes. Certainly, this is a "catch 22" that defies logic.

There are varying possibilities that a society may advocate--between treating people exactly equally or relying on them to totally take care of themselves because of the importance of liberty--the freedom to do what one will. None of the advanced societies are all one or all the other—all liberty or all equality. The Nordic model gives much more credence to the idea of equality.

Everyone deserves the help of society to develop to one's fullest potentials and therefore be one's happiest. The United States is far more on the side of liberty and the responsibility of everyone to take care of himself. But there are provisions by national, state, or local governments to take care of the poorest through food stamps, Medicaid, subsidized housing, etc. Of course, everyone is entitled to free education through the public schools. The realities however are that the schools are not equal. Private schools, which may be better, or public schools in richer areas are far more likely to be more effective.

While equality of opportunity is generally heralded as a goal of modern societies, in reality it is never achieved. Children of the rich have great advantages through: preschool, primary school, tutoring, summer camps, traveling, secondary education, and no financial strains to getting a college education in the best universities and to whatever level of graduate school to which they might aspire. Even beyond education, they might well have access to influential business people and to any necessary financial needs that might be necessary in developing a business.

Norway, as many European countries, has free university education. This gives qualified students the opportunity to pursue the careers of their choice.

**Who Owns the Natural Resources?**
In Norway, the society owns the oil. In Saudi Arabia, the king owns it. In America the capitalists own it. In Norway 95 to 100% of the oil profits go into the

"Oil Fund." This fund, now topping a trillion dollars, is earmarked for Norwegian pensions. Sometimes the government takes 1% to 5% to balance the budget.

In the U.S., in 2017, ExxonMobil had a gross profit of $75 billion. Its expenses, including $1.2 billion in income tax, left it with a $20 billion net profit. What if that $20 billion were put into the government's coffers because it was owned by the government in a welfare state like Norway? And Exxon is only one of the big four Oil companies in the U.S.

### Concern for Citizens--Welfare States

We can certainly surmise that in ancient civilizations the family or clan was concerned with its membership. In the larger societies the slaves, serfs, and other marginal people were not important in the concerns of the government. Whether it was religion or the magnanimous monarch who recognized a need to take care of the poor, around 1600 some laws were passed in England to take some care of the poor.

It is possible that the equalitarian thinking of some of the Enlightenment philosophers along with the advent of democracies following the American and French revolutions contributed to the assumption that we were all somehow equal. If we are equal, perhaps our needs should be a concern of our governments.

Europe has led the way in developing various welfare aspects of their countries. Free education through the university level, national healthcare, adequate pensions, paid vacations, and childcare leaves are only a few of the possibilities of the welfare state. Norway has all of these, and more.

The U.S. has pensions, which are often inadequate. It has free education through high school. It has some provisions for the care of the ill and disabled. Healthcare, paid vacations, and subsidized childcare are usually the province of the employers.

Making money for managers and stockholders seems to be primary in the U.S. Even in education at the various levels, administrators are not only paid more, but they seem to proliferate beyond their needs. Teachers and professors, who should be the major concerns in the education of students, are generally in the same straits as the workers in the factories. Managers obviously are more important than the doers

# CHAPTER 2
# A LOOK AT NORWAY

**Government**

Looking at the American presidential election of 2016, we find that President Trump received 46.09% of the popular vote. Hillary Clinton received 48.18%. Neither of these would have been sufficient to become the leader of the country in Norway. They would have to bring enough parties into the coalition so that a majority of the voters would be represented. Of the other American political parties: the Libertarian Party got 3.28% of the vote, the Green Party got 1.07%, the Independent Party got 0.54%, and the Constitution Party got 0.15%.

In a parliamentary government, the Libertarians might have gone with Trump, but that wouldn't have been enough to get 50%. The other two parties might've gone with Hillary, but it wouldn't have been enough to reach 50% either. The solution would have to be another vote.

In parliamentary elections, such as in Norway, the party attempting to develop a coalition will promise certain ministerial posts and agenda concerns to the other parties. That wouldn't work in America where the administrative branch, the President, appoints all of the ministers—the Secretaries of each department of the administrative branch.

Parliamentary governments have no elected administrator or president. They often have a king or queen that is the nominal head of the government. The primary leader is the Prime Minister, usually the leader of the most influential party—although he or she can be a leader of a smaller party in the coalition. (Kjell Magne Bondevik was a recent minor party Prime Minister in Norway.)

In Norway in the 2017 election, the Labor Party got 27.4% of the votes and 49 seats in the parliament. The Conservative Party got 25% of the votes and 45 parliamentary seats. The Progress Party, the furthest to the right, got 15.2% and 27 seats. The Center Party got 10.3% and 10 seats. And the Socialist Left got 6.0% and 11 seats. The Liberals got 4.4% and 8 seats. The Christian Democrats got 4.2% and won 8 seats, the Greens got 3.2% and 1 seat. The far left Red Party got 2.4% of the vote and 1 seat in parliament. 86 seats are needed for a majority.

The present government is made up of the Right Party, the Progress Party, and the Liberal Party. This gives them 80 seats. The Christian Democrats did not want to be part of the coalition, but achieved some favorable promises on the agenda if they would vote with the coalition.

Recently there was a question as to whether the Christian Democrats would support the new planned budget. Their leader didn't want to. If they did not, the government could fall and a new coalition could be formed with the Labor Party. This was proposed by the party leader. But many in the Christian party don't like the pro-abortion stance of the Labor Party, so they had a party meeting and voted 98 to 90 to go fully into the existing right-leaning coalition. The party leader resigned. So, the government coalition remained intact. My goodness, it almost sounds like the "fire and fury" in the American White House!

Parliamentary governments may be checked by an independent judiciary. The American way is to have three major branches of government. These, theoretically, are checks and balances against the excess of power by one or two branches. But, as we have seen recently in the United States, all three branches can be controlled by one party. When this is true, checks and balances are often non-existent.

### Ethics in Government

In Norway recently, the vice chairman of the largest party was accused several cases of harassment some years before. He resigned his position in the pa stayed in the party and continued to hold his seat in Parliament. It headlined newspapers for weeks.

A high-ranking member of the far-right party was a minister. He visited 1 with this Iranian girlfriend without permission from the Prime Minister. He also t his official government phone with him. This was enough to force his resignation fi his ministerial job.

In the US, a presidential candidate can brag about "grabbing pussies" and have a number of extramarital affairs, and his evangelical voters will support him. can lie thousands of times and his religious supporters will still support him. as lon; he says he is against abortion. But abortion is not mentioned in the Bible. There some Biblical Commandments that he seems to continually flaunt. Playing golf on Sabbath, bearing false witness against his predecessor, or indulging in adultery, e though commands from Sinai, are really clear.

I saw an interview with one of Trump's evangelical supporters. She said that behavior was between him and God. As I understand it, God has already spoken these behaviors. But possibly the great negotiator can show the all-knowing God error of his thinking!

When the Norwegian government makes a law, it is followed. You do not di and drive in Norway. You can lose your license and spend two weeks in jail. Last y at Christmas time the police set up roadblocks to catch drinking drivers. They stop 2000 cars and found one person whose pass the breathalyzer test.

### The Economic System

Socialism and the "welfare state" are often confused. While they both are based somewhat on the political ideals of "equality" and "equality of opportunity," Socialism attempts to reduce or even eliminate the power of the capitalists. The welfare state's objectives are two-fold: it attempts to increase equality of opportunity through reducing child and adult poverty and it fosters free education to the limit that a person can profit from it. You can see the contrast between the U.S. where rich kids have no financial problems in attending college, while lower and middle class students must both borrow and work to pay for their educations.

A few years ago I watched a TV interview with the young man at a Tea Party gathering. The interviewer asked him what he thought about socialism. He said, "I'm against it." Then the interviewer asked him what socialism was, and he replied, "I don't know, but I am against it."

"Socialism," like "love" has many meanings. Lenin, assuming that the state should own all of the means of production, said that, "socialism means from each according to its ability to each according to his work." In other words, you get paid for what you do and there are no capitalists to take most of the money. Lenin, of course, was trying to fit socialism between capitalism and communism, which Marx said was, "from each according to his ability, to each according to his needs."

There are other definitions of socialism. It might mean:

- ➢  When the government owns all of the means of production,
- ➢  When the government owns the major means of production,
- ➢  When the government owns some of the major means of production,
- ➢  When the government controls some of the means of production,
- ➢  When there is no private property.

So, socialism must be defined, and even practiced, before we can criticize it, or extol its glories. Norway owns some of the means of production, such as: oil and gas, transportation (the railroads, the buses and trams, and part of the airline system of Scandinavian Airlines, which is jointly owned with Denmark and Sweden.)

Capitalism, as criticized by Marx, allowed the person with the money to do whatever he wanted with his businesses. Unions grew to foster the interests of the workers-- so a bit of balance was achieved. The rise of democracy, with its emphasis on political equality, has forced laissez-faire capitalism to be regulated, rather than demolished, in more recent times.

Social democracy, or democratic socialism, is another economic possibility in which democratic governments regulate businesses, attempting to balance the positives for the capitalists and the general public.

Norway, along with its Scandinavian neighbors Sweden and Denmark, has elements of socialism and social democracy as its economic foundation.

America, by contrast, has some socialistic aspects. Social Security is somewhat socialistic in that people contribute according to their abilities and are granted retirement and disability pensions based on a portion of their needs. Medicare and Medicaid are more communistic, according to Marx, in that people contribute accordingly their abilities (paychecks) and are given medical care according to their needs up to a maximum amount. But because the government then contracts it out—it is capitalistic, in that the health insurance companies make money on the contract.

The insurance companies determine the co-pays and deductibles that will apply to the person who is insured. So, while the individual and the employer pay to the government, the government hires capitalistic companies to handle the details. The CEOs and stockholders thereby benefit from the government's protecting them from losses and guaranteeing them profits.

Actually the U.S. has a number of socialistic endeavors. The government owns a number of entities including: The U.S. Postal Service, Amtrak, and the lending agencies Fannie Mae/Freddy Mac, just to name a few. There are also a number of banks and mortgage corporations that it owns in addition to:1he Tennessee Valley Authority, the St. Lawrence Seaway Development Corporation and the Securities Investor Protection Corporation. It also may be the major lender to essential government projects, like Hoover Dam. At the beginning of the recession in 2008, President Obama loaned many billions of dollars to General Motors and

Chrysler. Much was paid back—but not all. The government may have lost over $10 billion in the deal.

### Gender Equality

Gender equality has been sneaking up on us for centuries. First it was the powerful queens like Maria Teresa of Austria and Elizabeth of England. Then some women, like Marie Curie in chemistry or Benjamin Franklin's sister in medicine, came along. Then the suffragettes came along demanding the right to vote. Nothing aided the feminist movement as much as contraception and abortion. More women went to the universities—in fact women are now over 60% of college students in both the U.S. and Norway.

Norway passed The Gender Equality Act in 1978. Revisions have been done since. Public boards and committees must have as close to half of the members of each sex as possible. So, a male soccer committee of 7 members would have to have at least three females, and a female soccer committee of 7 members would have to have at least three men.

The affirmative action for boards and committees only echoed the societal actions that had been occurring. It is seen in political parties, in the workplace and in the home. Two recent prime ministers have been women.

The prime minister, finance minister, the heads of the three parties in government are all women, as is the head of the very powerful Employees Association. Women are close to parity in the public sector but in private sector business only 15 of 213 businesses are headed by a woman. Still Norway is ranked second best of 144 countries in the World Economic Forum's Gender Gap Index for 2017, in a list dominated by the Nordic countries and Rwanda. The USA is 49th.

### Taxes

Income tax laws in both countries allow some deductions. Norway allows: a personal exemption, interest on one's residence, childcare expenses, and some travel business expenses. The USA allows those deductions and many more. Once you have your taxable income, Norway has a flat tax of about 25%. Then it adds 1% for income exceeding $20,000, 2.4% for income exceeding $30,000, and 22.5% for income exceeding $60,000.

America has a lower income tax. If you are single, the taxable income rate is: 10% up to $9,525, 12% from $9,525 to $38,700, 22% from $38,701 to $82,500, 24% from $82,501 to $157,500, 32% from 157,501 to $200,000, 35% from $200,001 to $500,000, and 37% above $500,000.

Norway also has a wealth tax 0f 0.15% on the total wealth of a person if it exceeds $200,000.

It also has a 25% consumption tax (a value-added tax or VAT-- like a sales tax) on goods and services. The VAT on food is 15%.

National insurance (Social Security) 8.2% for individuals and about 15% for employers.

Few people like to pay taxes, my wife excepted. And it is important to be in command of the country, both parties promise to go easy on taxes, but the Republicans make their case of promising middle class tax cuts. So, the middle-class voters elect them. Then miraculously the greatest beneficiaries are the wealthiest people and the corporations who were the major donors to the party. Of course, the wealthiest people pay the most income taxes.

Presidents Reagan, George W. Bush, and Donald Trump have all promised, then delivered, tax cuts. All borrowed from the Social Security and other retirement funds to pay for them. The government annually pays interest to the funds and promises to pay the pensions of those whose pension contributions were borrowed. By 2023, at the latest, Social Security contributions and the interest that the government pays are expected to be less that the total pensions paid. The pensions will then be partially paid by decreasing other government expenditures or by increasing taxes. Many expect that the pensions will be reduced.

More than 50 percent of the Trump tax bill's benefits will go to the wealthiest 5 percent of Americans, and more than 25 percent to the wealthiest 1 percent, according to the <u>Institute on Taxation and Economic Policy</u>. As *Businessweek* put it, "President Donald Trump and Republicans sold their $1.5 trillion tax cut as a boon for workers, but it's becoming clear just two months after the bill passed that the truly big winners will be corporations and their shareholders."

While Norway has no debt, The U.S. has over $20 trillion in debt. Every American owed $65,000 on that debt when Trump took over. Now there is an additional $3,500 for the trillion dollars that the Trump tax cuts cost. We can view that $68,000 in debt as taxes that should have been paid but are still owed. So, the apparent lower taxes of America are a sham. If the balanced budget Constitutional amendments finally pass, politicians will no longer be able to pull the wool over our wallets.

Property taxes often take a big chunk of Americans' outlay. This isn't true in Norway. My present one-million-dollar apartment in Oslo has a property tax of $800. I will be moving next month two miles away to Baerum. They have no property tax.

The point is that we must look at all taxes, not just income taxes. Tariffs levied against goods from other countries are really paid by the consumer. So, it is a hidden tax. Most of the cost of gasoline is state and federal tax. Excise taxes are included in the cost of goods, like alcohol. Then there is the cost of health insurance. It is not a tax, but it is an expense that most countries include in their taxes. The important question is—what do we get for what we have paid.


### Cost of Living

Because of the higher taxes, the cost of living is much higher in Norway. As examples, we can see that the cost of gasoline is generally eight dollars or more per gallon. This is about $2 higher than the rest of Europe, and more than twice what Americans are paying.

A pint of domestic beer in a bar would be about nine dollars. A meal in a cheap restaurant would be about $20. In the midrange restaurant about $50. Milk is about two dollars a quart, a dozen eggs about $4.50.

A 1/3 of a liter bottle of water would be about four dollars. (I could never understand why Norwegians would buy water—their tap water is right off the glaciers and is incredibly good!)

Transportation for a month of unlimited tram and bus journeys is about $90. (This is a lot cheaper than driving your car!) For those over 65 it is only $45 a month.

But taxis are expensive, $10 or more to get in and about a dollar for every 600 yards. A Volkswagen Golf or an equivalent new car would be about $40,000.

A one month fitness club membership would be about $50.

Private childcare is about $400 per month. State-run childcare (kindergarten) is about $240 per month. And the facilities are open from 7AM to 5PM.

A one-bedroom apartment in the city would be about $1200 per month. This is not that much different from US, at least in California.

### Religion

In Norway, 70% of the population belong to the state church, which is Lutheran. In 2017, the church was officially separated from the state. In the big cities, people are not particularly religious. In fact, a population survey last year found at 39% of the Norwegians did not believe in God. 37% did. The rest were unsure.

Since it has been traditional to have your children baptized in the church. This makes them an automatic member. With the separation of the church from state, and with a simplification of the way one can leave the church, the enrollment in the state church is tumbling in the cities.

Just under 3% of Norwegians are Catholic and another 3% are Muslim. 2% are members of the Humanist organization. All receive some financial support from the government.

Some religious holidays are also national holidays. Christmas Eve, Christmas, St. Stephan's Day (the day after Christmas), Easter, Easter Monday, Ascension Thursday, Maudy Thursday, Good Friday, and Whit Monday (the day after Pentecost). That only leaves 2 secular holidays—Labor Day and Constitution Day.

Thank God for religion!!

### Charity

Many Americans seem to be motivated to give more by the deduction allowed from their income taxes. Church contributions and clothes given to the Salvation Army can reward the donor with cash as their income taxes are determined. Norwegians get no such deductions. Can you believe that some people give to charitable causes because of a feeling of empathy?

The Salvation Army has placed clothes collection receptacles throughout Oslo. The concern for others is not only the concern of the government!

### The Environment

Norwegians are outdoor people who enjoy the mountains, lakes, fjords, rivers, trees, the snow, the sunshine—and whatever else Mother Nature's blessings bestow. Any threat to nature riles the population and its government. Whether it be the threat of war, the encroachment of housing on their sacred woods, or the threat of climate change—Nordmen are the first to take up the challenge with money, work and the zeal that their ethos germinates.

When electric cars hit the market, legislators let them be sold tax free. Charging stations appeared at spots where the cars might be parked. Apartments and homes soon installed them.

While American oil magnates and their legislative lackeys denied the scientific proof of global warming, in the name of laissez faire capitalism. Norwegians boarded their bikes, drove their electric cars and worked to reduce the greenhouse gasses that they had been producing.

There is a saying that "Norwegians are born with skis on their feet." During the long dark winters, lighted ski trails weave their ways through the forests. On the winter week-ends thousands of Nordmen, and Nord-women and Nord-children, spend the days skiing, snow picnicking, and enjoying the frozen gift of their latitude.

But every season has its fascinations. In the spring the trees and bushes come alive with leaves and buds. Summer is the time for hiking or biking the paths that were skied in the winter. And since the days are 24 hours of sunlight and dusk, and since most summer workdays end at 3PM—there are many hours to enjoy the summer daylight.

## FAMILIES

### Having Children Who Are Wanted

The anti-abortion value choice is obviously a religious one. Religions need more babies to save their souls so they can go to heaven. It doesn't hurt that they will also tithe their way to paradise.

Progressive Norway places its prime value on its society—with the welfare of the people as foremost. The conservative U.S. puts religion high on the list, along with making money, with the average citizen far down on the list of legislative priorities.

This is not to say that all Norwegians approve of abortion. The small Christian Folk Party has many who, for religious reasons, disapprove of abortion. But, as you know, our values can be derived from what we think our God wants, what is good for the society, or what a person wants.

When women say "I want to control my own body," this is a "self" centered value base. Those who want to follow the opinion of Pope Pius IX take a God-based value base. And, there are those who believe that unwanted children are not good for their country. This may be because every child contributes to climate change by producing $CO_2$ or by eating methane producing cows. Since increasing global warming is bad for the world society this would be deciding this value issue on a societal basis.

It is my observation that the year of "parental leave," in which both parents must participate in order to get the maximum number of months of paid leave, is essential in the child binding with both parents. And with at least one parent with them during that year, they should feel that they are loved. Because of contraception and abortion, we can assume that most of the Norwegian children are wanted.

After the first year, most children are involved in nursery school, which the Norwegians call kindergarten. Here again, they are nurtured by caring teachers and are in small groups of similar aged children where they can learn the importance of each one as an individual.

In America, by contrast, the child may not be wanted, because abortion was not allowed. Even if wanted, may stay home with one parent, or if both parents work, be placed in a daycare facility within a few weeks of birth. There is not the opportunity to bond with both parents in those early months. The daycare facilities in the U.S. will likely have a number of children in one class. This is necessary because most childcare options are private moneymaking businesses. So the little rascals are supervised, but perhaps not socialized effectively.

### Parental Leave

A survey of 196 countries found that only four had no federally financed parent leave. You guessed it! The good ol' US of A was one of them. So if there is to be any leave, the states or the employers must decide on it.

America does plenty of things well, but paid parental leave isn't one of them. Out of the world's 196 countries, the US is one of only four that has no federally mandated policy to give new parents paid time off.

Norway has some of the best parental leave laws. Mothers can take 35 weeks at full pay or 45 weeks at 80% pay, and fathers can take between zero and 10 weeks depending on their wives' income. It is common for fathers to take at least a month of "papa leave." That first year of child leave is paid by the government.

Other European countries vary in their laws. Finland, for example, starts maternity leave seven weeks before the expected birth. The mother then gets four more months and the father eight more weeks. Sweden gives 18 weeks to mothers, 12 weeks to fathers, then about 38 weeks to either parent. Iceland gives three months leave to each parent, then another three months to either parent. They are paid 80% of their salary while on leave.

### Subsidized Daycare

In Oslo, it is common to see a dozen three and four-year-olds with three teachers wandering through the woods, taking the tram--which is free for them, visiting parks and playgrounds and other areas. They are not restricted to a home or a small playground, as is normal in the US. Norwegians are always within a mile or two of forests, rivers, lakes, fjords and other domains in the home of Mother Nature. I have never seen people who are so enthralled with the wonders of the outdoors. In summer or winter, the call of the wilderness is universally heeded. Walking, running, biking, or cross-country skiing are the methods, wonderment is the attraction. And it all starts when the children are only wee ones.

## WORK LIFE

Norwegian laws are worker-friendly. Trade unions protect the workers in most occupations, including in the education systems and the healthcare areas.

### Wages

The minimum wage set by the federal government in the U.S. is $7.25 an hour. About half of the states meet this minimum. Georgia is a little over five dollars an hour, while in the District of Columbia it is about $12.50. Norway has no minimum wage, but the minimum paid to workers and farmers is about $20 an hour. The average monthly salary, after taxes, is about $3500.

**Vacations**

Four weeks of paid vacations per year are mandated. One extra week after age 60 is common. A check for vacation pay, of 10 to 12% of the yearly earnings, without the normal tax deductions, is paid before the vacation is taken. This allows all employees to be able to afford their vacations.

A common way for Norwegians to take vacations is by all-inclusive charter flights. Charter tours can be very inexpensive 3 to 5-star hotel facilities. Most Norwegians vacation in Greece, Spain or Portugal.

## Healthcare

Americans pay 40 to 50% more than any other country for their health care, but the World Health Organization rates that American health care as the 38th best in the world. Is this what Senate majority leader Mitch McConnell means when he said "it is for the good of the American people." Health care was certainly not on Donald Trump's list of things needed to "make America great again."

Many people were upset with the cost of their health care. They should be! But the problems include that:

> The health insurance company lobbies fight against a national government-run program because it would eliminate their profits for stockholders and their highly-paid administrators;
> The malpractice insurance companies do not want a cap on malpractice awards—it would reduce their premiums;
> Doctors must pay high malpractice insurance premiums to protect themselves from both legitimate and fraudulent claims—this increases what they must charge patients;
> Lawyers' lobbies worked to allow unlimited malpractice awards, even if the doctor was not really at fault;
> Many rich people don't want their taxes raised to pay for middle class and lower class health care, so lobby against it.

Research shows that many Congressmen hold large amounts of stock in health insurance and pharmaceutical companies, and many have close relatives (often their wives) on health care boards of directors.

The government is now the major customer of the private insurance companies. It hires them to operate many programs, such as Medicare. Why would they want a nationally operated health care system as we have in the Veterans Affairs nationally operated hospitals? There are no stockholders so no profits for insurance companies.

Obama wanted a federal insurance option and a cap on medical malpractice awards to bring down doctors' premiums which should reduce their charges,' but laissez faire capitalism won out. So, what was called Obamacare was not what he wanted—but he got his foot in the door for an eventual change to what all other advanced countries already have—a national healthcare program.

But Americans, according to many legislators and private health insurance companies, do not want the advantages of a welfare state. We are capitalists who firmly believe that health insurance companies' profits are far more important than the average citizen's health.

Health care costs will continue to rise in every country as life spans increase and diseases are conquered. It would be much cheaper if more people would avail themselves of earlier medical practices—a witch doctor's spells and potions or voodoo dolls and pins. These are far cheaper than modern medical care.

Another reason that witch-doctoring was less expensive is that primatives didn't have ambulance chasing lawyers ready to sue the shaman if an unexpected evil spirit incapacitated the incantation. But good luck on getting rid of the attacking ambulance chasing attorneys who add huge amounts to doctors' and hospitals' cost of doing business because of the insurance they must buy.

Seventy-year-olds generally have more experience with organ problems than ten-year-olds.  Maybe we should cut off free medical care for those who have retired!

Have you ever listened to older people sharing their medical problems?

"My Bach is aching."

"I can't get a Handel on my shoulder pain."

"I could make a long Liszt of my problems."

A conversation among the elderly is surely an "organ concert."

All other advanced countries have a socialized system to cover all or a large part of medical expenses, with no problem regarding pre-existing conditions. Taxes must be raised for this to happen, but the total amount paid by the middle-class and poorer citizens from their paychecks would be minimized. The total amount that they would pay out would be about half of what they pay now. Taxes would be higher but health insurance premiums would disappear.

In Norway you choose your own family doctor. Visits cost $20. If you need a specialist, the co-pay is $40. When your yearly doctor and prescription bills total $200 you get a free card that covers all doctor visits and prescription medicine for the rest of the year.

Here are some examples of medical charges:

--An MRI (magnetic resonance imaging) can cost $2,600 in the USA. The cost in Norway is $25 with a prescription at a state hospital, or $400 at a private clinic.

--Cost of a knee replacement in Kansas is $29,000, in Colorado $40,000, in Norway free.

--Cataract removal surgery in Alaska is $8000, in Florida $2300, and in Norway free.

--Cost of a colonoscopy in California ranges from $1200 to $7200. You guessed it,--free in Norway

Most doctors work Monday through Friday. but clinics are open every day and night around the city.

Another factor that reduces medical bills is that in Norway medical school is free—as are all universities. It is not uncommon for American doctors to finish their studies and internships owing $400,000 in government loans.  Unless they marry well, these loans must be paid off with higher bills to their patients

If you are handicapped so that you can't take public transportation, your doctor can apply for a taxi card. You get 70 taxi trips in a year locally. You pay $6 no matter what the bill is. (Taxi fares are very high in Norway. Fares start at $10 to $15.) The trips can be to the market, the doctor, or the opera—it doesn't matter!

Hospitalization, including ambulance, is totally free.

The realities of our outdated and expensive medical delivery system were made clearer to me yesterday in a conversation with an orthopedist and sports medicine doctor in Westlake Village. He had been the team doctor for some teams I had been associated with. He would like to semi-retire, working only two days a week—but he can't. It would cost him more than he would make. He either has to retire totally or continue full time. Why? His malpractice premiums are $50,000 a year. His daily overhead expenses are $1500. That covers: rent, utilities, insurance, salaries, etc. One salary is for a fulltime insurance clerk. In Norway, he wouldn't need the insurance clerk or the malpractice insurance.

Yesterday in the Norwegian newspaper Aftenposten, there was a story about a man who was treated for prostate problems. He died. In the U.S., it would have been a multi-million-dollar case, with the lawyer pocketing 35 to 50% of the award. In Norway, it is assumed that the doctors were following procedures and that it was just bad luck. So, no malpractice suit.

### Factors Keeping American Medical Costs So High

Healthcare in America costs much more than socialized medicine beca capitalism is more important to the lobbies and the legislatures they control than are needs of the citizens. All of the healthcare interests: doctor's groups, health insura lobbies, lawyer's lobbyists, pharmaceutical lobbyists, hospital lobbyists, etc.-- f financial interests in how healthcare is administered. In socialized medicine, most of hospitals are government-owned and most of the doctors are government educated employed.

It is the profit motive of our healthcare interests that keep the American health costs at 40 to 50% higher than in a socialized healthcare system.

The CEOs of the 70 top healthcare systems (including health insura pharmaceuticals and malpractice insurance companies) made a total of $9.8 billion, ju few years ago. Much of their pay is in stock options, so the amount of profit made by company directly affects the pay of the CEO. The median yearly household income in U.S. in 2015 was $56,515. The average CEO makes this much in a day. The average C pay has been about $28.5 million a year.

The CEO of UnitedHealth Group earned $279 million last year, while the CE( Cigna was just under $142 million, and the CEO of Anthem it was $48 million. But not just the CEOs who are in the multi-million-dollar range. For example, Anthem li the pay of its non-executive chairman as $18 million, the president of the business divi: earned $5.6 million, the chief financial officer was at $5.4 million, and the commer president at $5.4 million. Not everyone at Anthem makes millions. Many of the cler staff work for only $14 an hour.

Obama tried to reduce health insurance executive pay in the Affordable Care but the 2017 Trump tax bill more than restored the Obama cuts.

When you read the financial report of a company, such as Anthem, the salaries all included the expenses of the company. After all expenses, Anthem showed a profit share of $1.11 per share and there were over 258 million shares.

Its total revenue was $84.9 billion. From that you subtract the payouts, its expen all of the salaries, including the multi-million-dollar salaries of the executives, and

have earnings of $2.5 billion. Anthem paid only 22% of its earnings to the stockholde₁
about $550 million.

If just that fraction of the federal insurance that Anthem handles were sociali:
all those multi-million dollar salaries would be replaced with federal salaries if $200,
or less and the $2.5 billions in profit would be available for improved services or woulc
into funding the program or into the general fund..

But it is really not quite that simple.

IF Obama's federal insurance option were law, doctors would still have to
insurance clerks to bill the government, which would increase their overhead.

To have effective health coverage as they have in Norway, would probably req
a Constitutional amendment. There are just too many requirement for our legislator
agree upon.  Here's what would probably be needed:

- Doctors would have to be educated free so they don't start in practice owing
nearly a half million dollars.

- Lobbyists for health care would have to be eliminated—but that would inter
with free speech rights as the Supreme Court has recently ruled.

- Since it costs an average of a million dollars to run for the House of
Representatives and six million to run for a Senate seat, the government would have to
fund campaigns and no outside contributions should be allowed. This would run afoul
the previously mentioned free speech rights.

- The right to choose one's own primary care doctor should be preserved, as it
in Norway.

- Private health care facilities and insurance should be available, as in Norwaγ

So, you can see that the chances for reducing health care cost and of simultaneoι
increasing the quality of the American health care system so that it equals that of Euɾ
or Canada is very, very slim. As long as money is more important than people—just
Console yourself that "it is fore the good of the American people." I am sure that M
McConnell would approve!

## Education

Education starts in kindergarten which begins at age one. As soon as the
children can walk they socialize with both boys and girls. At age 3 or 4 they take the
buses and trams to parks, forests, and lakes. They learn to appreciate nature.

When they enter primary school at age 6 they begin to learn English, general
studies of religions, and the typical meth and social studies curricula.

Middle school starts at grade 7, as is common in the U.S. It is common to
learn German, French, or Spanish, along with the continued studies in Norwegian
and English.

In the recent PISA international education testing, Norway ranked 17, the
U.S. 31st.

The school year is from mid-August until the end of June, so their school
year is 6 weeks longer than the typical U.S. school year, but they have an extra two
weeks of holidays in that year.

Since they graduate from high school after grade 13, their total school time
is 13 years plus 13 more months of school attendance because of the longer school

year. So at high school graduation their total time in school would be about two and a half years longer than an American high school graduate.

As is common in Europe, a bachelor's degree is generally three years, a master's two more, and a doctorate three more. The graduate degrees are generally research degrees. Not too many courses, but lots of research experience.

Education is free at all levels. The government pays the transportation cost of students who are not within walking distance of their school. A neighbor of mine is a taxi driver who is paid $250 per day for transporting a middle school student from his home several miles in the forest where his parents operate a café that hikers and skiers use for rest and refreshments on their forays into the woods surrounding Oslo.

## Transportation

In order to discourage driving, to aid in the minimizing of $CO_2$ emissions, public transportation is very cheap but driving a car is expensive. Gasoline is generally $8 to $10 a gallon. The toll to enter Oslo is $5. Parking fees are required on streets in many areas. Public garages may charge $6 to $10 per hour. Even shopping malls usually charge, sometimes giving the first 2 hours free.

Public transportation runs often and inexpensively. Trams and busses are "on the second" in terms of their schedule.

## Recreation

The typical Norwegian relishes recreation. Summer is for hiking and biking. Winter is for play in the snow. Cross country skiing with the family, trekking to one's winter cabin, and downhill skiing are the favorites. It is common for middle class Norwegians to own a boat, a summer cabin by the beach, or a winter cabin in the mountains. Some have all three.

### Sports

It is no surprise that Norwegians dominate many winter Olympic sports, especially in the skiing events. But they have won many gold medals in the Summer Olympics and in European and world championships. One current bit of pride comes from the athletics accomplishments of three brothers in the 1500 meter run in the European Championships. In 2012, the oldest brother won it. In 2016, the middle brother won it. Then in 2018 the 17-year-old youngest brother won it—with the oldest brother 4th and the middle brother 12th.

About half of Norwegians are members of a sports club. Skiing, soccer, and team handball are among the most popular sports. You can find just about every sport being played somewhere. American football, rugby, cheerleading, sand volleyball are among the sport club activities. Sport in high schools and colleges is not subsidized. There are no scholarships.

Elite level world class athletes may be subsidized by the state. They also have paid coaches and top level facilities available to them.

Children are encouraged to play many sports. But high level competition is not allowed before reaching 12 years of age

# CHAPTER 3
# LET'S TAKE A LOOK AT TAXES

It is conceivable that America's taxes could be revised and not have income and Social Security taxes as the primary sources of revenue. So, let's take a look at some options.

Taxes commonly come from: personal income tax, corporate profits, social security taxes (including pensions and healthcare), property taxes, goods and services taxes, excise taxes, and wealth and inheritance taxes. The percent and types of each tax vary considerably from country to country. For example, in New Zealand and Australia there are no Social Security taxes, they are included in the income tax.

The U.S. gets 40% of its revenue from personal income taxes, and another 9% or 10% from corporate taxes. Under Trump's recent tax cuts these will be reduced. The average sales and service taxes (VAT) is 24% for OECD countries, which includes the United States, but they are much higher in most of the world. In the US, Social Security taxes amount to about 24% of tax revenue. In the OECD, the average is 26%. Some Eastern European countries and Japan are in the 40% range.

Sales taxes, such as value added taxes (VAT) in the U.S. are only about 25% to 35% of what is common in the rest of the world.

Property taxes are much higher in the US, about 10% of total revenue, compared to 6% in the OECD countries.

Revenue from different sources in the OECD countries includes taxes for the national government as well as for municipalities and states. The amount of taxes collected as a percent of the federal budget for other OECD countries and the U.S. are:

| Type of tax | OECD | U.S. |
| --- | --- | --- |
| Income tax | 24% | 39% |
| Social insurance Social Security | 26 % | 24% |
| Corporation taxes | 9% | 8% |
| Consumption taxes (VAT, sales | 33% | 17% |
| Property taxes | 6% | 11% |
| Other taxes | 3% | 1% |

Recently in the US, the top 1% of earners earned 17% of all income and paid almost 37% of all income taxes. Their average tax rate was 24%. For the top one-tenth of 1% of earners, almost 140,000 people, their average income was $4.4 million and their average tax bill was over a million dollars. The total revenue earned through income taxes was nearly $150 billion. This does not seem fair to me since about 45% of Americans don't pay any income tax. However, if we look at how the rich made their money, many of them made it because of the government, through contracts, favorable tax breaks, and so forth.

While the personal exemption has been doubled under Trump's tax plan, many popular deductions are reduced or eliminated like: state and local income tax, casualty losses, unreimbursed employer expenses, home equity loan interest, etc. But the child care credit is increased to $2000. In addition, home mortgage interest has been adjusted to cover only the first $750,000 of home value. If you are rich, your estate and gift taxes will be exempt to a large degree.

While the rich will still pay most of the taxes on incomes, they can pass on to their children just about all of their wealth. Some of the new tax provisions are smoke and mirrors. For example, take the child tax credit. It would be deducted from the taxes you owed. But 45% of Americans don't pay income taxes, so it does them no good. And what is the point of giving a credit for children, when the world has too many of them!

### FINANCIAL REALITIES TO PAY FOR OUR GOVERNMENT

Governments may support themselves these three ways:

- ♦ **Immediate taxing--of their incomes, sales, property, etc.**
- ♦ **Delayed taxing--by borrowing or devaluing their currency**
- ♦ **Socialism--by partial government ownership of some industries**

In the U.S. we use the first two, because we are one of the most capitalistic countries in the world. Still, we are rated 19th in the United Nations' annual happiness ratings and 23rd in our perception of corruption in government. Might that be because capitalists spend millions of dollars annually to get legislators to enact into law what they want, like lower taxes and fewer regulations designed to allow them to ignore the well-being of the citizens?

Nearly 200 years ago Alexis de Tocqueville observed that, "A democratic government is the only one in which those who vote for a tax can escape the obligation to pay it. (Democracy in America, Chapter 13)

And regarding government ownership, the happiest countries borrow less, but use some degree of socialism—allowing earnings, that would go to individuals in the U.S., to be used for the general good—a welfare state. For example, during the corona virus scare, Norway was loaning companies money at very low rates, or taking stock in those companies. The money came from its trillion dollar savings account earned from the government owned oil company. The account was to be used to guarantee pensions and when needed by the state—such as the economic crisis that grew out of the COVID-19 pandemic. On the other side of the Atlantic, the U.S. had to borrow the funds it needed, indebting every American another $6060. So much for state ownership!

As with democratic republics throughout the world, the people who have been elected to pass the laws usually have more than the normal amount of money—and are not likely to pass laws that negatively affect their financial status. Self-centered values win out over comprehensive societal values. Secondly, the major corporations, whose financial oxen would be gored by equitable taxation. Consistently bribe the legislators through financial gifts for lower taxes or other desires. Be that as it may, let us suggest some ideas for possible just taxation.

Many billionaires today have made their own fortunes through their own entrepreneurship. Bill Gates—with Microsoft, Warren Buffett—with his business enterprises, Sergey Brin and Larry Page— with Google and Alphabet, Carlos Slim—with his extensive businesses in Mexico, and Oprah Winfrey— with her many ventures, have all made huge fortunes through their intelligence, work ethics, and senses of purpose. Why not keep their taxes relatively low while they live, then taxed heavily when they die?

# CHAPTER 4
## SUGGESTED PRINCIPLES  OF FAIR TAXATION

1. Everyone should earn the money that they have as their own "wealth," so eliminate inheritances. This is essential to realize the ideal of "equality of opportunity." Equality of opportunity requires that no one start life with significant advantages over other people. This would eliminate any inheritance tax breaks.

2. People shouldn't have children until they can afford them. We might tax pregnancy, then return the full tax, plus interest, when the child starts school.

3. Taxes should be based, as much as possible, on how they are used. (For example: roads and bridges from auto and gasoline taxes; business taxes on trade and similar expenses; consumer taxes on schools; income taxes on general government expenses, etc.)

4. Corporations should be taxed at as low a level as possible to bring more corporations into the country to create jobs and to increase revenue broadly. International corporate tax rates, that are actually paid after all business deductions are taken, are generally within a 3% to 4% range of each other. So unless you have a very large company, it may not make a great deal of difference where your corporation is located. Deductions are often so liberal that some major companies do not pay any corporate taxes. There should be a very low flat corporation tax rate based on gross profit.

A flat rate on the business done in each country, rather than a tax in the home country of the corporation—which might be a tax haven or a low tax country, would be fairer.

5. There should be no deductions or exemptions to a flat tax—which should be much lower than today's rates.

6. Sales and value added taxes should be paid to the municipalities or states where the buyer shops. In 1992, the Supreme Court exempted Internet sales from many such taxes. The loss of tax revenue is estimated at $34 billion. The Court is revisiting this issue this year.

7. Pensions must be fully funded by workers' and employers' payroll taxes, then they should be secure—without the government allowed to borrow from the fund.

8. All income should be taxed at the same rate: no capital gains, all stock trade gains, gambling winnings, etc. With no deductions for losses or expenses. Whatever way we make money there are almost always negative factors. If you work ten miles from home, you drive your car or take the bus. You use your time to travel, but don't get paid for it. This negative, which is an essential for your economy can certainly be compared with other negatives people encounter when making money: like selling stocks at a loss or picking the wrong horse at the racetrack. And capital gains tax rates on stock trading or the selling of property, at half the rate of tax that a worker pays—is a special advantage to the wealthy. Possibly we should reverse it

and have people who earned money from the sweat of their brow pay half the tax that a capitalist pays! Only kidding! But why shouldn't all income be taxed the same?

9. Any institution collecting money, including private schools and colleges, churches and charities could pay 10% in taxes. Since numerous studies have shown that some charities are far more efficient than others in their use of donations, a non-partisan committee could award the tax income from all charities to the most efficient and worthwhile charities or educational institutions. All charities will still have 90% of their pre-tax income to use as they will.

10. Tax greenhouse gas producers to aid in reducing global warming. Tax plastic and other products that increase global garbage-- or products, like paper, that reduce global forests. Taxing greenhouse gas use would apply to many users, such as: gasoline and coal use, cement (a major polluter), electricity produced by polluting fuels, beef and other animal foods and dairy products, since they emit methane and use water, etc. With the amount of plastic in the oceans equaling the weight of the fish—non-biodegradable plastic should be taxed high.

11. When infrastructure is needed, or repairs are needed, tax those who get the benefit of the facilities. So, gasoline and diesel taxes and automobile or truck excise taxes and registration fees would be the sole source of funds for road repair and building, bridges, etc. Electric vehicles, while good for the environment, still use roads and bridges so appropriate taxes on car registration, batteries or electricity need to be found. These should be less expensive than fossil fuel taxes.

If new airports are needed or personnel are needed to handle aviation, tax new airplanes, the yearly registration of the planes, etc. And, tax the tickets. The same would be true of railroad and public transportation means.

12. Unhealthy substances or activities might be taxed higher, such as: sugary drinks (as in UK), tanning salons, tobacco, alcohol, other psychoactive drugs, and some entertainment.

# CHAPTER 5
# LET US TAKE
# A QUICK LOOK AT PENSIONS IN THE
# DEVELOPED COUNTRIES.

Most people have a combination of their nation's retirement program, like Social Security, and a private plan through an insurance company or tax-deferred plans, like a 401(k).

In the United Kingdom, retirees receive about 29% of what they made when they were working--as their pensions from the state (equivalent to Social Security in the US). This puts many of the over-75s into the poverty class. That 29% pension compares with an average of 63% of in-state pensions in other OECD countries, which range as high as 80% in Italy and the Netherlands. United Kingdom workers and other Europeans often rely on privately purchased retirement insurance. In the UK, the private pension assets are $2.2 trillion, which is equal to about 95% of their GDP.

Some countries are even higher in the amount of pension fund insurance, such as: the US, Switzerland, the Netherlands, and Denmark. Once the UK's private pensions are added to the state pension, the average income in retirement for UK pensioners rises to just over 60% of their former career earnings, just below the OECD average. In the US, the average Social Security pension is 45% of what the retirees were earning. The average for the OECD countries is 63% of what they had been earning.

Had they contributed 9% of their income to a private pension fund annually, the U.S. retirees would have had total pensions of about 82% of what they had been earning. Many more Americans are working well past retirement age. This eliminates their reliance on Social Security, while it funds their trust account so that when they do retire it will be at a higher level. In some countries, this is not possible for state workers who must retire by age 70—as is often true in Norway.

Retirees in the U.S. are more often living in poverty than any other OECD country. It is about 22% in the US. Compare that with: the Netherlands at 2%, France at 4%, Canada at 7%, Germany at 9%, and the OECD average of 13%. In other countries, the pension contributions are higher and are generally supplemented by higher national taxes.

As you know, Social Security retirement now starts at age 67, but people are expected to live past 80. (When Social Security started, retirement was at 65 and the lifespan was 64. The government made money on that!) Because the government continues to borrow from Social Security to finance tax-cuts, it owes a great deal of money to the potential retirees.

The revenue exceeded the payments until 2010. That year $74 billion more was paid out than was deposited. The interest that the federal government owed the Social Security Trust Fund made up the difference. This will be true until sometime between now and 2023 when the Social Security payments will exceed its revenue and the interest that it is owed by the federal government. By about 2035 the present pension payouts are expected to decrease by about 25%. Social Security is one of the "entitlements" that many conservative lawmakers want to reduce or eliminate.

A campaign promise made by Al Gore when running for president was that he would not allow the government to borrow from the Social Security Trust Fund. But he lost, and his opponent borrowed $1.7 trillion from the fund to finance tax cuts for the rich and the war in Iraq.

In the US, because of the aversion to higher taxes, retirement is commonly underfunded. But luckily, we have low taxes! The current combined Social Security contribution is 12.4%, equally shared by the worker and the employer. If we assume you earned an average salary of $60,000 for 45 years, and assume 3% interest on your contributions, then add the interest, it would total about $343,000. If you were to live at your average salary it would last about 7 years. But if you averaged $60,000 a year, your final salary was undoubtedly over $100,0000 per year, so the savings would last less than four years at your final salary.

Let's continue with the above figures. Assume that you were born in 1950, worked 45 years, have a salary of $100,000 a year and will retire this year. Your monthly Social Security retirement check would be about $2,434, or $29,000 per year—just 29% of what you had been earning. You are now 68 and are expected to live 15 more years if you are a male and 17.5 years if you are female. Your contributions will last about 12 or 13 years (since your unused contributions will still be earning interest). The government will have to pay you $30,000 to $100,000 more than you contributed.

If your final yearly salary was $50,000, your contributions plus interest would be about $175,000. Your monthly check would be about $1,515—or $18,180 per year—36% of what you had been earning. Your contributions plus interest will last about nine and a half years, so the government will have to reach into its pocket and pay you $100,000 more than you contributed if you are male and $145,000 more if you are female.

As you can see, the way Social Security payments are determined gives lower income workers a higher percentage of their contributions than is true for the higher income workers. Do you think you might need retirement insurance—or should you work more years?

How can pensions pay for themselves? We either need a higher retirement age or higher pension contributions. But what legislators would vote for either, knowing that they would be defeated in the next election.

Even in autocratic Russia, when President Putin suggested increasing retirement ages for women from 55 to 63 and for men from 60 to 65—the people complained loudly. But in Russia there are only 2.3 workers per retiree. Not long ago it was 5 per retiree. It is expected to fall to 2 per retiree in five years.

It is obvious that in countries with low fertility rates, fewer will be in the workforce—unless immigrants are brought in to do the jobs. But this just kicks the can down the road. (These immigrants will eventually retire, unless they are brought in as guest workers with no chance if permanent residence,) Automation, 3D printing, robotics, and artificial intelligence will eventually take over most jobs, beginning with the lower level jobs. Consequently, retirement ages must be raised and people

must fund their own pensions. But how many will agree to this in a democratic
republic?

# CHAPTER 6
# WHAT DO AMERICANS REALLY WANT

Perhaps the United States should determine its basic objectives before working on its legislative endeavors. As has been mentioned, Americans pay nearly twice as much for their medical coverage as most countries, yet their medical delivery system is rated at about the 38th best in the world, the worst of any developed country. This is because private enterprise and stockholders must take their cut from the insurance premiums. Is it the duty of the American government to put private profits ahead of the public interest? What do Americans want?

Still another major concern is whether we should put present day concerns ahead of future concerns. Since the United States legislators and public think primarily of "now," the future is impacted. Year after year the federal deficit limit is increased to cover wars, tax reductions, or entitlement spending. Our national debt is one of the highest in the world as a percentage of our gross domestic product (GDP). Are we willing to reduce our future pensions to pay for this? Are we willing to have our children pay for our selfishness? Are we willing to have our dollar's worth less in the future? Are we willing to endure the future pains because of living beyond our means today? Why not? We do it with our credit cards!

An area to consider is whether we want happiness or low taxes. The U.S. citizens have been sold a bill of goods on low taxes. The U.S. has relatively low taxes (26% of GDP). These include: income taxes, excise taxes, sales taxes, gasoline taxes, import taxes, property taxes, business taxes, inheritance taxes, and a number of less visible taxes.

These low taxes have brought: a crumbling infrastructure, poor roads, short or no vacations, expensive childcare, pension contributions that are too low to fund adequate pensions. Then our contributions have been borrowed by the government to fund tax reductions for the rich, wars, and the softening of recessions. This borrowing has increased the gross national debt to the highest in the world and the percentage of debt to the gross domestic product, (the amount of goods and services produced in a country in a year), to the sixth worst ratio of the developed countries. Every person in the U.S. owes more that $68,000 on that debt. About $3,500 was added recently to pay for the Trump tax reductions for businesses and millionaires. Did your family's benefits from the tax breaks exceed $3500 per member? If so you were lucky. If not, somebody else was lucky at your expense.

## Happiness or Low Taxes

For those of you who are interested in some of the factors used in determining the "happiness" rankings in the United Nations' 2018 summary, here are a few: the median GDP per capita (median is the exact middle person in the society. The median income for one person in America is $18,000. (Median income for a family of four is $61,000.) Contrast this with the mean or average, which is the total amount earned nationally, divided by the population which is $54,000. The average earnings are inflated when all the billionaires' money is averaged in.

Norway by comparison has a median income for individuals is $30,000 and an average income of $65,000. Median income for a family of four is $104,000. Its median income is the highest in the world. The U.S. is fourth in the world.

### Happiness Criteria

Median income is only a part of the "happiness criteria," the others are: social support, freedom to make life choices, healthy life expectancy, perceptions of corruption, and one's propensity to be generous.

In 2018 Finland ranks number one, followed by: Norway, Denmark, Iceland, Switzerland, Netherlands, Canada, New Zealand, Australia, and Sweden. Israel was 11th, Costa Rica 12th, United States 18th (having fallen from 12th a few years ago) and Ireland 15th (rising four places from last year's survey). Germany was 16th, United Kingdom 19th, Mexico 25th, Singapore 26th, France 31st, Russia 49th, Japan 51st, Hong Kong 71st, China 79th, Pakistan 80th, Venezuela 82nd, Greece 87th, Somalia 93rd, South Africa 101st, India 127th, and Central African Republic last at number 155.

The U.S. has dropped from 14th in 2017, and 11th a few years ago. Apparently making America great again is also making it sadder!

The happiest countries are also rated very low in government and business corruption, which is a major factor in determining the happiness of citizens.

### International Taxes

Here is a quick glance at some tax facts.

The total taxes paid (income, social security, value added taxes), as a percent of GDP, are: Denmark 49%, France 48%, Finland 44%, Sweden 43%, Norway 42%, Iceland 38%, Greece 36%, New Zealand 37%, Japan 32%, Canada 32%, Turkey 30%, Switzerland and Australia 28%, the United States 26%, Ireland 24%, and Mexico 18%.

### Another Glance at Socialism

Americans have an aversion to socialism and communism. But what are they? One definition is that in communism the government owns all of the means of production, and in socialism, the government owns the major means of production. But in practice there are few illustrations of these definitions. For example, in Norway, the government owns: the postal system, the airports, the major airline (along with Sweden and Denmark), the hospitals, a number of other businesses, and the liquor stores. It has part ownership in: oil and mining companies, theaters, some banks, research facilities and a number of other enterprises. These provide much of Norway's employment and the profits go into reducing debt, rather than into the pockets of capitalists as in the so-called capitalist countries. There are, of course, many multimillionaire business people in Norway. These often own shipping companies, hotel chains, super markets, and many other businesses. In fact, there are more billionaires per billion people in the democratic socialist countries Norway, Sweden and Iceland than in the U.S.

# A Major Problem with American Democracy
## Elections

When two political parties hold all the power in a democracy, as in the U.S., non-democratic politicians will do what they can to energize their voters and to suppress the voting rights of the opposite party. Power, not democracy or justice, is the goal. Both parties have been guilty, but of late the Republicans have won the "crooked mile" race. Led by the greatest political liar in American history, others have followed suit. In the recent mid-term election, Brian Kemp, a candidate for governor of Georgia, told a crowd that the Democrats had hacked the voter registration system. He had no evidence. He was also the attorney general of the state, and as such, was responsible for the election. Ho hum—that's democracy as it has devolved in parts of the U.S.

The New York Times had counted over 5,000 lies and misleading statements during the first ten months of 2018. In that same Georgia race, Trump said that Kemp's opponent would take Georgia backwards. What did he mean "Backwards?" It has the $7^{th}$ lowest high school graduation rate in the country at 70.4%. It has the $19^{th}$ lowest median income. Did he mean back to slavery? Hardly likes since the person he was criticizing was a black lady!

In several states the Republicans in power have developed voter IC programs aimed at keeping likely Democratic leaning voters from the polls. Perhaps the greatest affront to democracy in the recent Republican gerrymandering.

Such practices would never even cross the minds of the Norwegians or any other Nordic peoples. Their international reputation for honesty and for the democratic process is unassailable. That is why Norway is rated as the best democracy in the world.

Multiple parties in the Norwegian government, as in most European governments, practically assure that no single party has all the power.

Another option is called Ranked Choice Voting (RCV). San Francisco, Oakland, Santa Fe, and Minneapolis are municipalities that are using this type of voting. It has been shown to increase voter turnout. Each voter ranks the candidates. If one person has a majority, that's it. If not, the candidate with the least votes is removed from all ballots and the process is started again, until there is a winner. RCV eliminates run-off elections, so is cheaper for the government. It also allows minor parties a real chance because voters will not think they are wasting their votes on a non-electable candidate because their major party candidate could be ranked second.

The state of Maine now has RCV through a referendum. Republicans fought it and the governor and legislature refused to enact it. So, a new referendum passed with even more votes, so now it will be used. Please shed a tear for the politicians, who lost out to the citizens!

### Gerrymandering

The party in power in a state can reorganize its voting districts so that areas with large opposition voting blocs are put into one irregularly shaped district while the surrounding districts give the party in power majority districts. This is called gerrymandering, after Governor Gerry, in the early 1800s in Massachusetts, who first designed such irregular boundaries for congressional districts. In fair elections, the voters choose the politicians. In gerrymandering the politicians choose the voters.

A few weeks after the 2016 presidential election a federal court in Wisconsin ruled, in a 2 to 1 decision, that the Republicans had unconstitutionally drawn partisan gerrymandered districts to take away legitimate voting rights of Democrats. The decision is being appealed to the US Supreme Court. The Supreme Court of Pennsylvania ruled that the Republican gerrymandered districts were unconstitutional. In February of 2018 the US Supreme Court let the ruling stand.

The Supreme Court has ruled a number of ways in gerrymandering cases. In 1964, in Reynolds v. Sims and Wesberry v. Sanders by 8 to 1 majorities, the court ruled that states were required to draw their districts in equal measure according to population. None of this, however, prevented districts from being drawn along partisan lines. In cases in which black voters were gerrymandered to reduce their voting clout, the Supreme Court generally protected them—but not always!

To give you an idea of some extreme differences in state and federal elections, a few years ago:

—Connecticut had one house district with 191 people; another had 81,000.

—In New Hampshire one township with three people had a state assemblyman; the same as another district with 3,244 people. The vote of a resident of the first township might therefore seem to be about 1,000 times more powerful in deciding state issues.

—In Vermont, the smallest district had 36 people, the largest had 35,000, again a voting-power ratio of almost 1,000 to 1.

—In Utah, the smallest district had 165 people, the largest 32,380 (196 times the population of the other).

—In the 2012 national election for the House of Representatives, more than a million more Democrats voted, but the Republicans won more seats, 234 to 201.

—In the same year in Wisconsin's state elections, 51% voted Democratic, but the Republicans won 60 of the 99 State Assembly seats—60%.

On May 22, 2017, in Cooper v. Harris, the Supreme Court ruled in a 5–3 decision that the 14th Amendment's Equal Protection Clause had been violated in North Carolina's racially based gerrymandering in two Congressional districts. In January of 2018, a three-judge federal court ruled that the Republican gerrymandering of the districts was unconstitutional. While Republicans represent about 50% of the voters, to the Democrats 46% to 48%, their gerrymandered districts give them 10 of the 13 House of Representative seats—77%. Here is North Carolina's 12th District—which is safe for Democrats.

If "one person, one vote" means anything and the legislators ignore it, an impartial Supreme Court should rule on this principle. But there's the rub! Supreme Court justices are nominated based on their points of view. They are confirmed based on their points of view.

So the checks and balances envisioned by the Founding Fathers is often a rubber stamp for the other two parts of the ruling Washington triangle. The triangle sometimes looks like a straight line— as it does in 2018.

Recent Republican redistricting in Wisconsin and obvious racial redistricting in North Carolina have convinced the Supreme Court to take another look at this political power- building practice. But the prime concern for any government is building a power base for its interests. Democracy? Ha!

The Supreme Court, in another Republican gerrymandering case, Gill v. Whitford, which is based, not on race but on political party preference, will examine the issue in its 2017–18 session. With a Republican majority on the Court of 5 to 4, will the right to gerrymander win?

The Supreme Court, in June of 2018, kicked two cases back to the lower courts. One was the Wisconsin case in which the Republicans had gerrymandered the districts so that while 53% of the votes were cast for Democrats they only received 40% of the state assembly. The other case was in Maryland, where the GOP won 41% of the vote and got 12% of the seats in Congress. The Maryland Democratic Governor admitted that the intent of the redistricting was to ensure that Democrats would be elected.

14 years ago, in a dissenting opinion, Supreme Court Justice David Souter warned that with new technology incumbents would be able to redistrict their states so that there were great dangers to representative democracy. The justices on the Court could not agree as to what was legal and illegal redistricting.

**A POSSIBLE SOLUTION**

Voters of both California and Arizona, through the initiative process, forced a popular vote on the method of redistricting. Naturally the leading political parties were against the proposed methods. What right do the voters in a democracy think they have, anyway! Legislators should have the ultimate authority to rig elections. It's like the divine right of kings. If God didn't want them to gerrymander districts She wouldn't have let them be elected!

The Arizona solution for federal and state representation is to have two Democrats, two Republicans, and one independent chair as the basic deciding group. Their general criteria are:

➢ That they are in compliance with the US Constitution and the Voting Rights Act, that districts are roughly equal in population,

➢ That they appear compact and contiguous,

➢ That they respect communities of interest,

➢That they incorporate visible geographic features; city, town, and county boundaries; and undivided census tracts,

➢ That they are electorally competitive as long as the aforementioned criteria are satisfied.

Former California governor, Arnold Schwarzenegger, a Republican, is one of the most vocal critics of this undemocratic practice, as is Barack Obama.

California's anti-gerrymandering law applies only to state offices. The legislature still draws the federal districts. There are three groups of commissioners: five representatives from each of the two major parties and four from neither party. A solution must have three positive votes from each group.

Another possibility that we might consider would be to utilize a computer program which would develop nearly square districts within the state that would be based on the population at the last census, and with the most populous district having no more than 5% of the number of voters in the least populous district. Arizona's requirements would be a good start for developing an efficient and fair program.

# CHAPTER 7
## A PEAK BEYOND THE OBVIOUS—WHAT MAKE US WANT OUR FORM OF GOVERNMENT?

As one who has studied psychology, philosophy, and political systems, I have hypothesized two spectra. Both deal with the psychological needs of individuals. But these individual needs transfer directly to how people will attach themselves to various political parties and how they will vote.

One continuum relates to individuals and stretches from the need for power and satisfying selfish interests to the unselfish ability to love and to feel empathy. We will define love the same as it is defined by Ashley Montagu in the Encyclopedia of Mental Health. "Love is a communication, to another person, of one's deep involvement in that person's welfare, of one's profound interest in him as a person, demonstrated by acts that support, submitted, and contribute to the realization of his potential in the fulfillment of his personality."

The word "love" is used in so many ways, usually meaning "I approve." "I love pizza," or "I love Tom Cruise," don't have the same meaning as Montagu defined the word. It is the unselfish meaning that we will use.

HUMANITARIAN LOVE       SELFISH INTERESTS

This continuum can be viewed as representing an individual or a society according to where they lie on the selfishness to unconditional love spectrum. The welfare states are closer to the left side of the continuum, the U.S. and counties like Saudi Arabia lie closer to the right.

### The Psychological Need for Power

While Freud emphasized the need to feel pleasure as the reason for how we act, his one-time friend, Alfred Adler, believed that we were motivated by a drive for power. Power was necessary because as infants we had none. We could not feed ourselves, talk, or change our diapers. We also may not have had enough cuddling to make U.S. feel that we were important. So we developed, what Adler called, inferiority complexes.

In order to feel important, we rely on a number of behaviors to get what we want as we grow up. When very young we may cry and yell when mother does not buy U.S. our favorite cereal in the market. We may bully a younger child who is not a threat to us when we are in elementary school or even high school. The same motivation for power will probably follow us into adulthood. Most people want "power over" others. Some are able to achieve the "power to" do something. That something might be to develop a business, to invent a gadget, or even to think our way into an adequate understanding of ourselves and our world,

Donald Trump is the most obvious example of needing to feel power over others that I have ever seen. But there are millions of others—they just don't have the high podium or the popular Twitter platform that he does.

Have you ever heard people gossiping about another? Have you ever heard about cyber bullying? Have you ever seen a parent making fun of a child who couldn't throw a ball or pronounce a word? All of these illustrate a feeling of inferiority by the parent and a behavior directed at making him or her feel superior to another with a resulting feeling of power!

On the other hand, have you ever heard about Albert Schweitzer or Mother Teresa or a Peace Corps volunteer? Have you ever witnessed a person doing something nice for a homeless person or another person in need?

The psychologist Erich Fromm, in his book the "Art of Loving," wrote that as we mature as loving people we go from selfishness, to recognizing that another person is also important, to the ability to unselfishly love one or a few people, to the generalized ability to love. He said that "we learn to love by being loved." The welfare states pursue this ideal.

A second continuum therefore illustrates where a person could fall on the need for power to the "ability to love" maturity scale.

Ability to love unselfishly    Need to use selfish power

You can see the development of maturity, as the ability to love, in some people as they grow psychologically. Bill Gates and George Soros can be seen as people who have arrived at the left side of the maturity scale. Donald Trump and the Koch brothers are among the majority who are stuck on the right side of the scale, still trying to overcome their inferiority complexes.

### Where Do Countries Stand?

It doesn't take a wizard to see that the welfare states of Europe lie closer to the left side of the scales. The U.S., African, Mid-East and South American countries are more on the right. A few South American politicians have promised a move to the left, but subsistence farmers don't produce enough excess wealth to spread around. Nearly all European countries top the USA in welfare spending even though the U.S. is the world's richest country.

Is it that Europeans are more loving to begin with, have European parents done a better job of raising loving children? Or has the idea of equality filtered down from the governments? Possibly the two world wars had something to do with it. A commonality of hardship may have moved the people into a more empathetic mood. Whatever it is, an attitude of sharing and caring is more common in Europe than in the U.S.—Hungary and Poland excepted!

Where should America be on these continua?

**Can we learn anything from Norway or other countries that are happier and have better democracies?**

www.ingramcontent.com/pod-product-compliance
Lightning Source LLC
Chambersburg PA
CBHW081954260726
48657CB00009BA/2923